SPACE

By Madeline Tyler

BookLife
PUBLISHING

©2019
BookLife Publishing
King's Lynn
Norfolk PE30 4LS

A catalogue record for this book is
available from the British Library.

ISBN: 978-1-78637-453-0

Written by:
Madeline Tyler

Edited by:
Holly Duhig

Designed by:
Daniel Scase

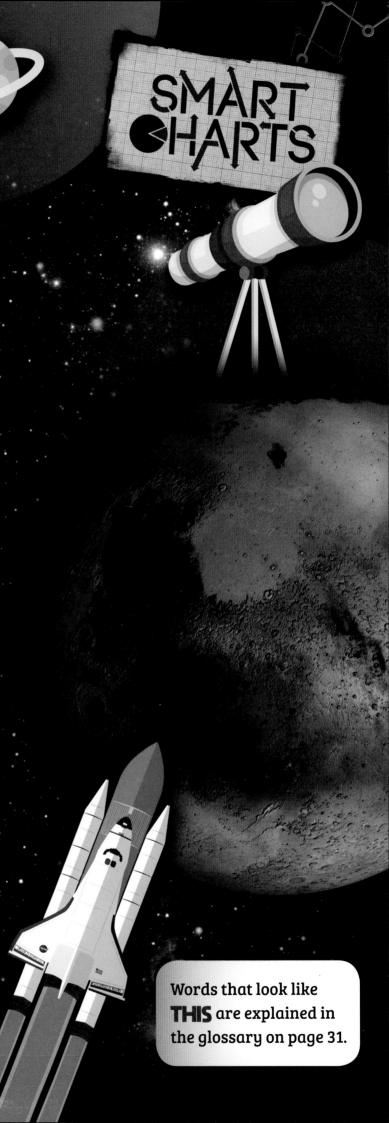

SPACE

SMART CHARTS

Words that look like **THIS** are explained in the glossary on page 31.

KNOW YOUR CHARTS!

WHAT IS DATA?

Data is another word for information. Data can be facts, numbers, words, measurements or descriptions. For example, someone might collect data about the different types of houses along a street. They might record how many houses there are, what colour they are, and when they were built. Data can be hard to understand, or **INTERPRET**, especially if it's a long list of words or numbers. Putting the data into a chart or graph can make it easier to read. Different charts and graphs are used to show different types of data.

TABLES AND TALLY MARKS

HOUSE COLOUR	TALLY	TOTAL
RED	⊬⊬ I	6
BLUE	I I I	3
GREEN	I I	2
BROWN	⊬⊬ I I I	8
YELLOW	I	1

Tables are used to write down data about different things. They are usually quite simple and have a few rows or columns. Tally marks are used to count things up. The tally marks can be recorded in a frequency table. This shows how many of each thing there is. Tally marks are drawn in sets of five to make them easier to count. You draw four lines and then the fifth one strikes through the others.

PICTOGRAMS

You can use the data from a frequency table to make a pictogram. Pictograms show the same information but with pictures or symbols.

RED	⌂⌂⌂	6
BLUE	⌂ ⌂	3
GREEN	⌂	2
BROWN	⌂⌂⌂⌂	8
YELLOW	⌂	1
	KEY: ⌂ =2	

BAR CHARTS

Bar charts usually show data that can easily be split into different groups, such as colours or months. You can easily compare the data in a bar chart and see which column is the highest.

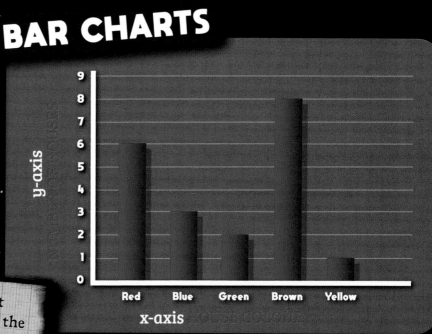

Graphs have two axes. The one that goes up and down is the y-axis and the one that goes left to right is the x-axis.

PIE CHARTS

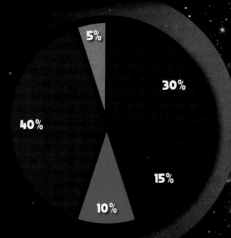

Pie charts are usually circular. They are split into different slices, just like a pie! Pie charts show data compared to the total number of something. For example, the total number of houses on the street is 20. Two of the houses are green – this is ten percent (10%) or one-tenth (1/10).

LINE GRAPHS

Line graphs show if there is a correlation (a connection or trend) between two sets of data. This line graph shows that there is a **POSITIVE CORRELATION** between the number of houses and time – the number of houses has increased as time has passed.

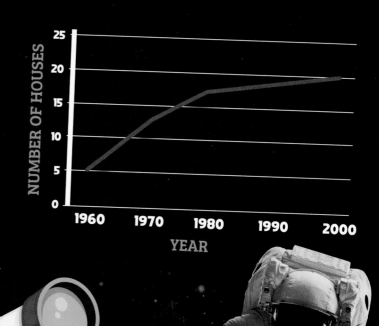

SPACE

Space is everything that you can see in the sky. It includes the Sun, the Moon, all the stars, and all of the space in between. In fact, most of space is actually made up of this 'empty' space between planets and other objects.

EXOSPHERE

600

THERMOSPHERE

Outer space is many kilometres above Earth. Between Earth and outer space is the ATMOSPHERE. Earth's atmosphere has several layers that stretch far into the sky. These are: troposphere, stratosphere, mesosphere, thermosphere and exosphere. The troposphere is the closest to Earth and the exosphere is the farthest. It's hard to say where exactly the atmosphere ends and space begins, but many scientists agree that space starts at around 100 kilometres (km) above Earth in the mesosphere. This is called the Kármán Line.

ALTITUDE (KM)

This only shows part of the exosphere. It's the largest layer in the atmosphere and is actually over 10,000 km thick!

HOW THICK ARE THE DIFFERENT LAYERS OF THE ATMOSPHERE?

TROPOSPHERE	STRATOSPHERE	MESOSPHERE	THERMOSPHERE	EXOSPHERE	
					0
					100
					200
					300
					400
					500
					600

THICKNESS (KM)

100

MESOSPHERE

50

STRATOSPHERE

20

TROPOSPHERE

10,000!

In 2012, two Canadian teenagers, Mathew Ho and Asad Muhammad, sent a LEGO man – the 'LEGOnaut' – 24 km up into Earth's stratosphere using a **WEATHER BALLOON**.

Space, or the universe, is huge. It goes on for thousands, millions, billions and trillions of kilometres. In fact, no one is completely sure how far the universe stretches. Humans have only travelled 400,000 km away from Earth, which is just a bit farther than the Moon. The farthest human-made object from Earth is a SPACE PROBE called Voyager 1. Voyager 1 was launched by NASA in 1977 and, since then, has passed by our solar system's two largest planets, Jupiter and Saturn. It has sent photos of both these planets, and their moons, back to Earth. Voyager 1 is now over 20 billion km away from Earth and is still going! Scientists are hoping that Voyager 1 will be able to teach us even more about our universe in the future.

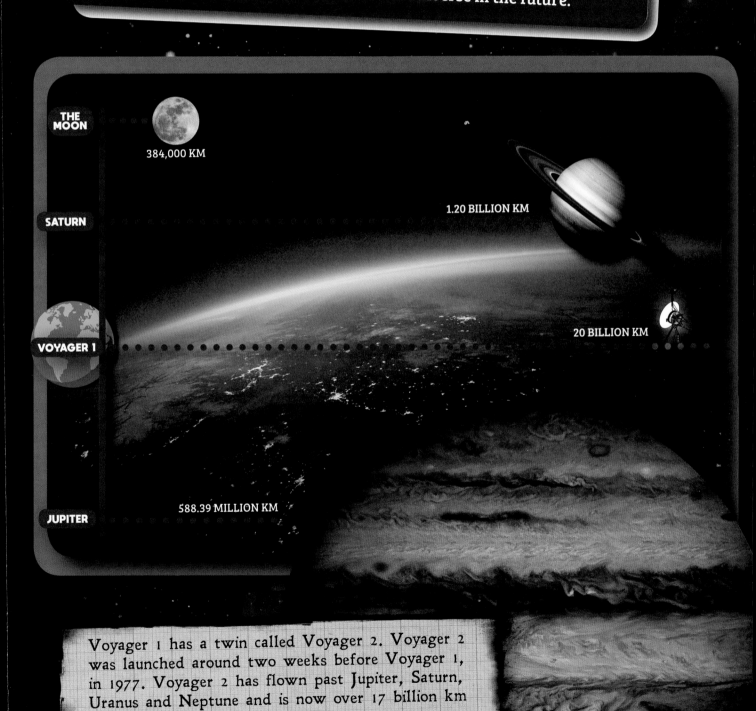

THE MOON
384,000 KM

1.20 BILLION KM

SATURN

20 BILLION KM

VOYAGER 1

588.39 MILLION KM

JUPITER

Voyager 1 has a twin called Voyager 2. Voyager 2 was launched around two weeks before Voyager 1, in 1977. Voyager 2 has flown past Jupiter, Saturn, Uranus and Neptune and is now over 17 billion km away from Earth.

THE BIG BANG

It's very hard to know exactly how big the universe is because it's always expanding (getting bigger). Many scientists and **ASTRONOMERS** believe that the universe began around 13.8 billion years ago with a huge explosion called the Big Bang. Before the Big Bang, there was no space, no time and no **MATTER**. Nothing existed before the Big Bang. As soon as the universe was created it expanded very quickly, from something very hot and **DENSE**, smaller than an **ATOM**, to the size of a city in less than a second. As the universe continued to expand, it slowly cooled over billions of years. As it got cooler, atoms, stars, and galaxies formed. The universe is still expanding, and there are now around 2 trillion galaxies in the **OBSERVABLE UNIVERSE**.

Go to page 13 to learn more about galaxies!

TIME BEGINS
(BIG BANG)

ONE SECOND

THREE MINUTES | 1 BILLION DEGREES CELSIUS (°C)

300,000 YEARS | 10,000°C

200-250 MILLION YEARS | -200°C

9 BILLION YEARS | -270°C

PRESENT DAY

Although we now know more about the universe than we've ever known before, there is still a lot that we don't know about. Some things may always be a mystery to us. For example, scientists know that everything that we can see is made up of atoms. Atoms are extremely small and are made up of even smaller **PARTICLES**. Atoms join together to make bigger things. You're made of atoms, your school is made of atoms, Earth is made of atoms, and even the Sun is made of atoms. However, atoms only make up around 4% of the entire observable universe, so what is the rest of the universe made of? Scientists call this mystery 'stuff' dark matter and dark energy. They believe that dark matter holds everything in the universe in place, and that dark energy pushes everything apart.

WHAT IS THE UNIVERSE MADE OF?

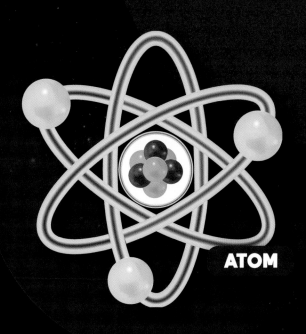

ATOM

- ● DARK ENERGY
- ● DARK MATTER
- ● ATOMS

STARS AND GALAXIES

BIRTH OF A STAR

If you look up at the night sky, you might be lucky enough to see lots of shining stars. Stars might look tiny from Earth, but they're actually some of the biggest objects in the universe. Stars are huge balls of hot, burning **GAS** that give off lots of heat and light. Not all stars are the same – they can be different sizes, colours and temperatures. Some stars may also be a lot brighter or denser than others, too. This usually depends on where a star is in its life **CYCLE**.

Stars are born inside nebulas. Nebulas are giant clouds of gas and dust. When nebulas shrink, they get very hot. Once they reach around 10 million °C, they explode, and a new star is created.

MAIN SEQUENCE PHASE ● OTHER

Stars spend around 90% of their life in the middle section of their life cycle – the main sequence phase – as main sequence stars.

ORION NEBULA

Stars burn a gas called hydrogen to produce heat and light. Eventually, all stars run out of hydrogen. When this happens, they die. Different stars die in different ways depending on their **MASS**. Large stars become red supergiant stars and then either neutron stars or black holes. Smaller stars become red giants, then white dwarfs and finally black dwarfs.

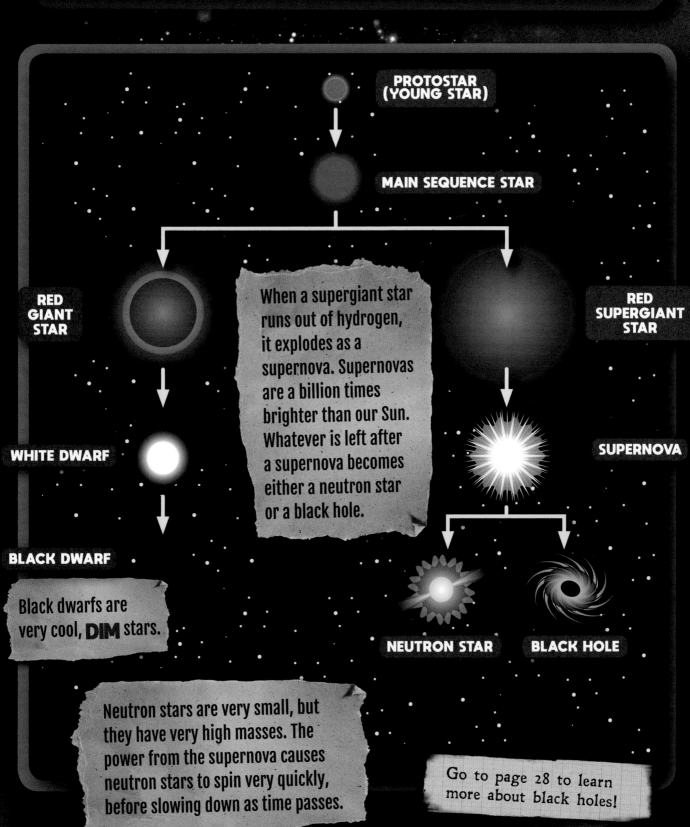

PROTOSTAR
(YOUNG STAR)

MAIN SEQUENCE STAR

RED GIANT STAR

RED SUPERGIANT STAR

When a supergiant star runs out of hydrogen, it explodes as a supernova. Supernovas are a billion times brighter than our Sun. Whatever is left after a supernova becomes either a neutron star or a black hole.

WHITE DWARF

SUPERNOVA

BLACK DWARF

Black dwarfs are very cool, **DIM** stars.

NEUTRON STAR

BLACK HOLE

Neutron stars are very small, but they have very high masses. The power from the supernova causes neutron stars to spin very quickly, before slowing down as time passes.

Go to page 28 to learn more about black holes!

TYPES OF STARS

The most common stars in space are main sequence stars. Some main sequence stars, such as blue giants, are very hot and very bright while others, such as red dwarfs, are small and cool. Red dwarfs are so dim that it's difficult to see them without using a telescope.

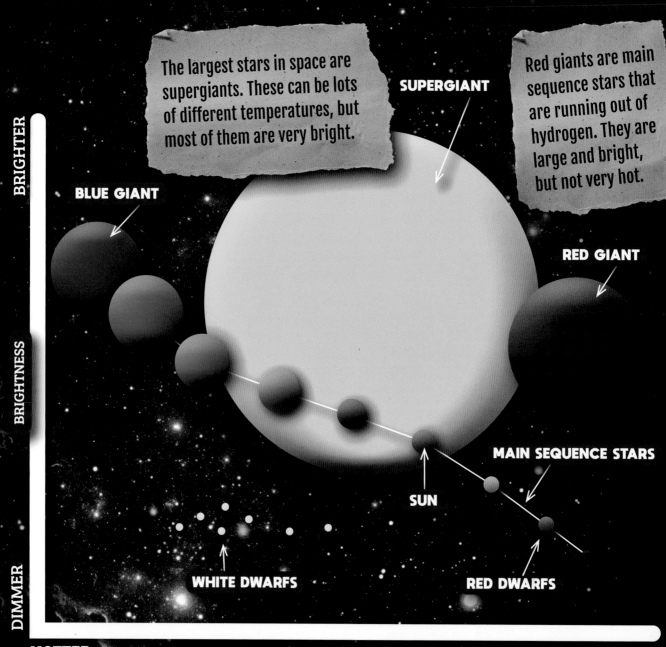

The largest stars in space are supergiants. These can be lots of different temperatures, but most of them are very bright.

Red giants are main sequence stars that are running out of hydrogen. They are large and bright, but not very hot.

SUPERGIANT

BLUE GIANT

RED GIANT

BRIGHTER

BRIGHTNESS

DIMMER

MAIN SEQUENCE STARS

SUN

WHITE DWARFS

RED DWARFS

HOTTER

TEMPERATURE

COOLER

Once they have run out of hydrogen to burn, some red giants eventually become white dwarfs. White dwarfs are very small, very hot and very dense, but they do not glow very brightly.

GALAXIES

A large collection of stars is called a galaxy. Some galaxies are small and only contain a few million stars, while others are much larger and might have around a trillion stars. Galaxies are usually full of lots of gas and dust too, which is all held together by a **FORCE** called **GRAVITY**. Galaxies are either spiral-shaped, **ELLIPTICAL**, or irregular. Spiral galaxies are the most common in the universe, and our own galaxy – the Milky Way – is a spiral.

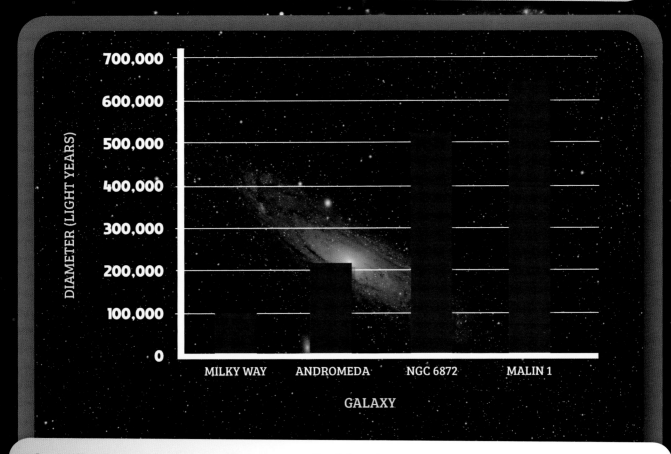

DIAMETER (LIGHT YEARS)

700,000
600,000
500,000
400,000
300,000
200,000
100,000
0

MILKY WAY   ANDROMEDA   NGC 6872   MALIN 1

GALAXY

The Milky Way is quite small compared with other galaxies in space. It's only 100,000 **LIGHT YEARS** across, while our nearest galaxy – Andromeda – is around 220,000 light years across. The largest galaxy ever found by scientists – IC 1101 – is an elliptical galaxy and it has a **DIAMETER** of roughly 6 million light years!

Elliptical galaxies are the largest galaxies in the universe. They can be egg-shaped or ball-shaped and usually contain mostly old stars.

THE SUN

Our nearest star, the Sun, is a main sequence star. It's mostly made of the gases hydrogen and helium, but it also contains a small amount of oxygen and some metals too. The Sun gives us heat and light and, without it, it would be far too cold and dark to survive on Earth.

Earth spins on its **AXIS**. The side of Earth that is facing the Sun is in the light, which we call day. The side that is facing away from the Sun is in the dark, so it's night-time. Earth travels around the Sun following a path called an orbit. The time it takes for Earth to complete one orbit around the Sun is called an **ORBITAL PERIOD**, or a year.

The Sun is extremely hot – the centre can reach up to 15 million °C!

WHAT IS THE SUN MADE OF?

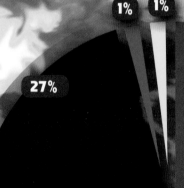

1%
1%
27%
71%

- HYDROGEN
- HELIUM
- OXYGEN
- METALS

A solar system is a collection of planets, **DWARF PLANETS**, moons and asteroids that all travel around (orbit) a star. The Sun is at the centre of our solar system. It's so large that its gravity has pulled eight planets, five dwarf planets, more than 170 moons and millions of asteroids towards it. The planets that orbit the Sun are Mercury, Venus, Earth, Mars, Jupiter, Saturn, Uranus and Neptune.

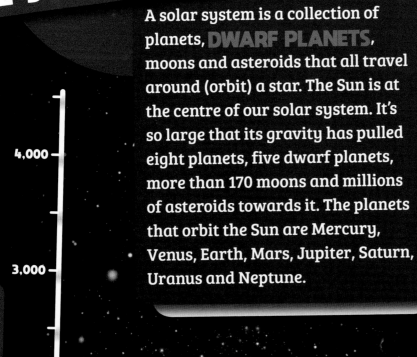

DISTANCE FROM SUN (MILLION KM)

4,000

3,000

2,000

1,000

NEPTUNE

URANUS

SATURN

JUPITER

MARS

EARTH

VENUS

MERCURY

1   10   100

ORBITAL PERIOD (EARTH YEARS)

It takes Earth 365.25 days – or one Earth year – to complete one full orbit of almost 150 million km around the Sun. Some planets' orbits are much shorter, while some are far longer. The farther away from the Sun a planet is, the longer its orbit is. Mercury is the closest planet to the Sun. Its orbit is almost 58 million km and takes only 88 Earth days. Neptune is the farthest planet from the Sun. Neptune's orbit is around 4.5 billion km and takes 165 Earth years!

This graph shows that there is a positive correlation between how far from the Sun a planet is and how long its orbital period is.

ROCKY PLANETS

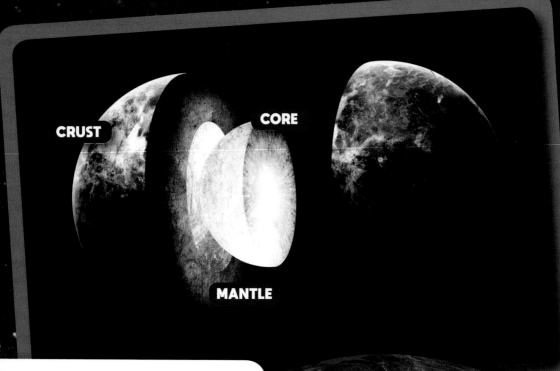

CRUST

CORE

MANTLE

The planets in our solar system are either rocky (terrestrial) planets or gas planets. The four planets closest to the Sun – Mercury, Venus, Earth and Mars – are rocky planets. The rocky planets are mostly made of rock and metal. They have a hot core surrounded by a mantle and a crust. The core is a solid ball of metal and the mantle is a layer of hot rock. The crust is a thin layer of hard rock that makes up the surface of each planet.

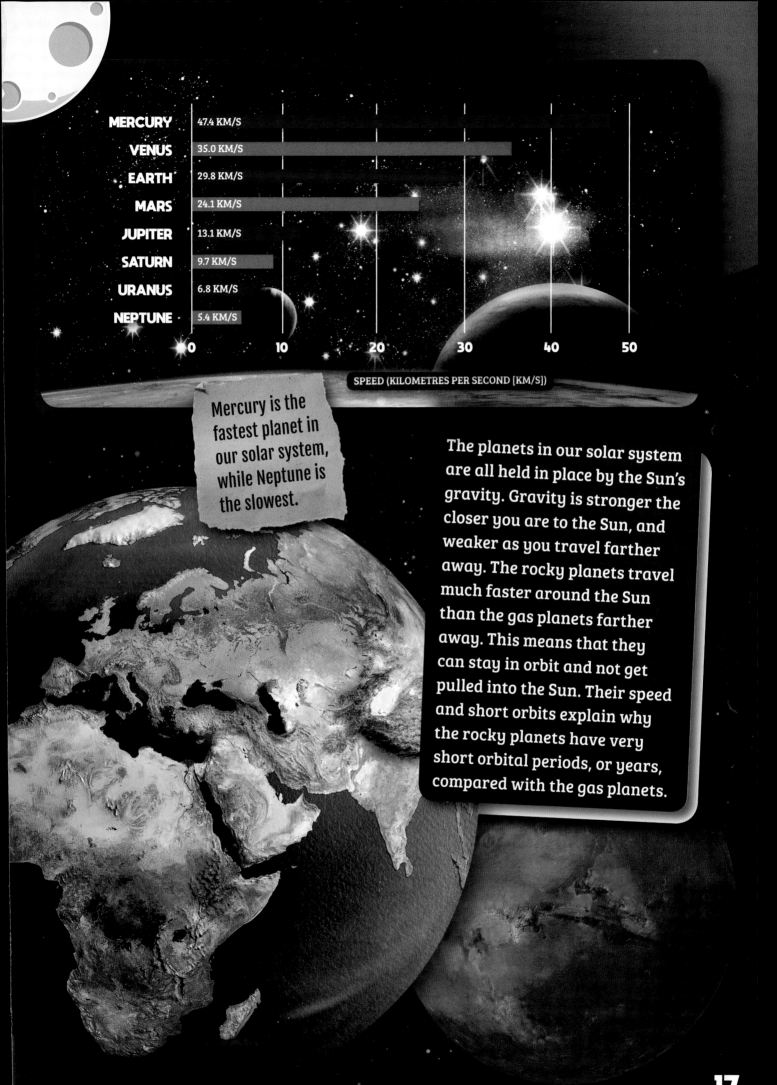

Planet	Speed
MERCURY	47.4 KM/S
VENUS	35.0 KM/S
EARTH	29.8 KM/S
MARS	24.1 KM/S
JUPITER	13.1 KM/S
SATURN	9.7 KM/S
URANUS	6.8 KM/S
NEPTUNE	5.4 KM/S

0   10   20   30   40   50

SPEED (KILOMETRES PER SECOND [KM/S])

Mercury is the fastest planet in our solar system, while Neptune is the slowest.

The planets in our solar system are all held in place by the Sun's gravity. Gravity is stronger the closer you are to the Sun, and weaker as you travel farther away. The rocky planets travel much faster around the Sun than the gas planets farther away. This means that they can stay in orbit and not get pulled into the Sun. Their speed and short orbits explain why the rocky planets have very short orbital periods, or years, compared with the gas planets.

GAS PLANETS

Jupiter, Saturn, Uranus and Neptune are the four gas planets in our solar system. They are much larger than the rocky planets, so they are sometimes called gas giants. Unlike the rocky planets, the gas giants are made of layers of gas and liquid that surround a small core made of rock and metal. This means that the gas planets don't actually have a solid surface, so it's impossible to stand on them!

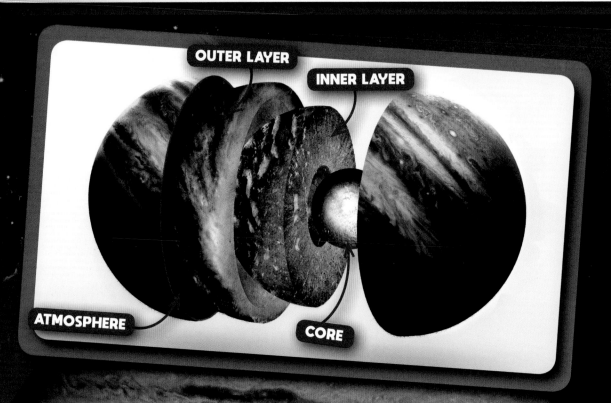

OUTER LAYER

INNER LAYER

ATMOSPHERE

CORE

Jupiter is the largest planet in our solar system. Both Jupiter and Saturn are made up of a small core of rock and metal, an inner and outer layer of liquid gases, and an atmosphere.

The larger something is, the stronger its force of gravity is. The gas planets are much larger than the rocky planets, and this means that their gravity is stronger too. In fact, their gravity is so strong that all four of the gas planets have dozens of moons as well as rings of ice and rock that orbit them. Saturn has the widest and brightest rings, which can even be seen from Earth with a telescope.

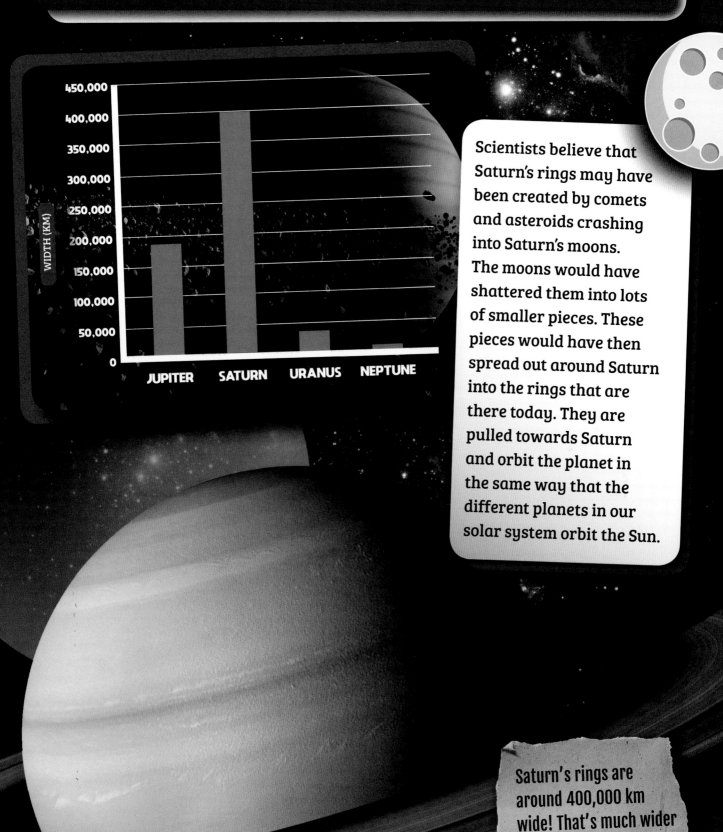

WIDTH (KM)

450,000
400,000
350,000
300,000
250,000
200,000
150,000
100,000
50,000
0

JUPITER   SATURN   URANUS   NEPTUNE

Scientists believe that Saturn's rings may have been created by comets and asteroids crashing into Saturn's moons. The moons would have shattered them into lots of smaller pieces. These pieces would have then spread out around Saturn into the rings that are there today. They are pulled towards Saturn and orbit the planet in the same way that the different planets in our solar system orbit the Sun.

Saturn's rings are around 400,000 km wide! That's much wider than Neptune's rings, which are only around 6,000 km wide.

Uranus and Neptune are the two farthest planets from the Sun and, because of this, they are also the two coldest planets in our solar system. Even though it's actually closer to the Sun, Uranus is colder than Neptune because of its cold core, which is around 4,700°C. This might sound very hot, but it's not even nearly hot enough to warm the whole planet. In fact, Uranus's core is surrounded by ice-like materials including water, methane and ammonia. Although they are still gas giants like Jupiter and Saturn, Uranus and Neptune are sometimes called ice giants because of their freezing temperatures.

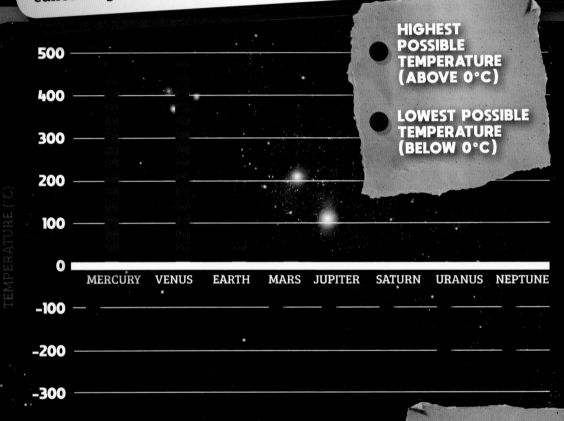

● HIGHEST POSSIBLE TEMPERATURE (ABOVE 0°C)

● LOWEST POSSIBLE TEMPERATURE (BELOW 0°C)

TEMPERATURE (°C)

500
400
300
200
100
0
MERCURY   VENUS   EARTH   MARS   JUPITER   SATURN   URANUS   NEPTUNE
-100
-200
-300

Unlike the rocky planets, temperatures on the gas planets don't change much across the planet or throughout the year.

As well as some extreme temperatures, the ice giants are also home to some other types of crazy weather. The fastest winds ever recorded on Earth were during cyclone Olivia in 1996, when wind speeds reached 408 kilometres per hour (kph) in Australia. However, this is nothing compared to winds on Neptune, which can reach over 2,000 kph! Not only is this the fastest wind speeds ever recorded in our solar system, it's also faster than sound travels on Earth!

WINDS ON EARTH					
SPEED OF SOUND ON EARTH					
WINDS ON NEPTUNE					
0	500	1,000	1,500	2,000	2,500

SPEED (KPH)

Rain is very different on the gas planets. Some scientists believe that the temperatures and pressures inside the ice giants are high enough to turn the methane gas in the atmosphere into diamonds. These would rain towards the planet's core to create a sea of diamonds.

The Giant Dark Spot was a huge storm on Neptune that was first spotted by Voyager 2 in 1989. The storm was the size of Earth but has since disappeared.

MOONS

A satellite is anything that orbits a planet or a star. Our planet, Earth, is a satellite because it orbits the Sun. Some satellites are launched from Earth to help with TV and phone signals. Anything that is put into orbit by humans is called an artificial satellite. Planets, which orbit a star, and moons, which orbit planets, are called natural satellites.

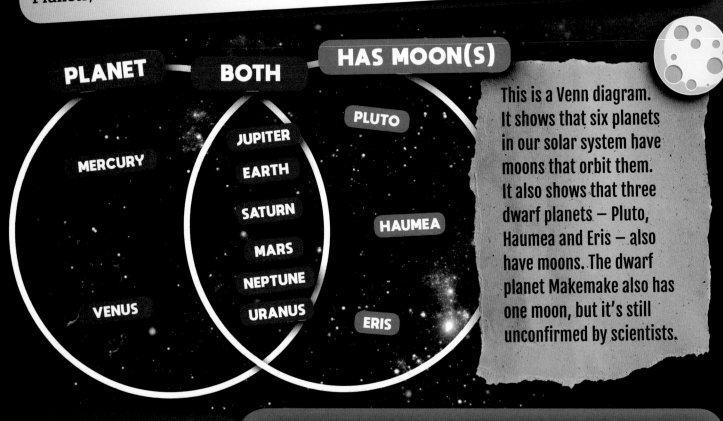

PLANET — **BOTH** — **HAS MOON(S)**

MERCURY

VENUS

JUPITER
EARTH
SATURN
MARS
NEPTUNE
URANUS

PLUTO

HAUMEA

ERIS

This is a Venn diagram. It shows that six planets in our solar system have moons that orbit them. It also shows that three dwarf planets – Pluto, Haumea and Eris – also have moons. The dwarf planet Makemake also has one moon, but it's still unconfirmed by scientists.

Some planets, such as Jupiter and Saturn, have more than 60 moons each. Some of these are unconfirmed, which means that they need to be researched more by scientists before they can be called 'confirmed moons'. Other planets, such as Mercury and Venus, don't have any moons at all. Earth only has one moon and we call this the Moon.

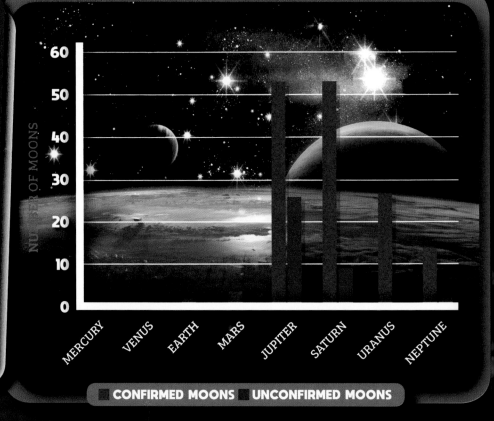

NUMBER OF MOONS

60
50
40
30
20
10
0

MERCURY VENUS EARTH MARS JUPITER SATURN URANUS NEPTUNE

■ CONFIRMED MOONS ■ UNCONFIRMED MOONS

THE MOON

Earth's only natural satellite is the Moon. It's much closer to Earth than any of the stars or planets in space, so it appears as a very large, bright circle above us.

Humans have been sending spacecraft to the Moon since 1959, when the Soviet Union crash-landed a spacecraft called Luna 2 on the surface. In 1969, the US became the first country to successfully land humans on the Moon. The astronauts Buzz Aldrin and Neil Armstrong were the first people to ever walk on the Moon, and some of their footprints are still there today. The last manned mission to the Moon was in 1972, but it's still the farthest into space that humans have ever been.

Although the Moon may look smooth and shiny from this far away, it's actually very rough and is covered in hundreds of **CRATERS** and mountains.

Although there have been many manned and unmanned trips to the Moon since 1959, still only 12 people have set foot on the Moon so far.

NUMBER OF PEOPLE

4

3

2

1

0

1959   1964   1966 1967 1968 1969 1970 1971 1972 1973   1976

YEAR OF LANDING

HUMANS IN SPACE

INTERNATIONAL SPACE STATION

During the first few trips to space, astronauts and **COSMONAUTS** only spent a couple of days there before returning to Earth. Now, however, they can spend weeks or even months up in space on board a special space station called the International Space Station (ISS). The ISS is the largest spacecraft ever built. It orbits Earth and contains everything that astronauts and cosmonauts need to live and work in space for long periods of time.

Because the ISS is so huge, it couldn't be launched from Earth – it had to be built in space! The first parts of the ISS were sent into space in 1998 and there have been people living on board since 2000, ten years before it was finished in 2011.

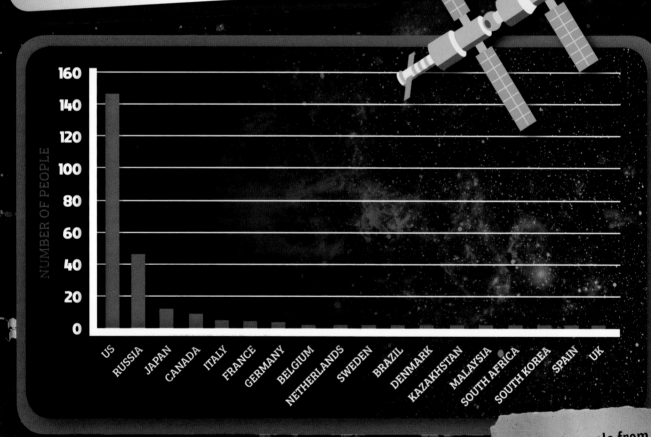

NUMBER OF PEOPLE

160
140
120
100
80
60
40
20
0

US RUSSIA JAPAN CANADA ITALY FRANCE GERMANY BELGIUM NETHERLANDS SWEDEN BRAZIL DENMARK KAZAKHSTAN MALAYSIA SOUTH AFRICA SOUTH KOREA SPAIN UK

Over 200 people from 18 different countries have visited the ISS. Well over half of these people are from the US and Russia.

The astronauts and cosmonauts living on board the ISS carry out very important experiments while they're up in space. They look at how the human body changes in space, how other livings things such as animals and plants survive, and what happens to different materials, including metals and crystals.

Most people spend a few weeks or months in space before returning to Earth. However, sometimes astronauts and cosmonauts have to spend much longer away from home and away from Earth. Valeri Polyakov holds the record for the most days in a row spent in space. Polyakov spent nearly 438 days on the Russian space station Mir. That's over a year in space!

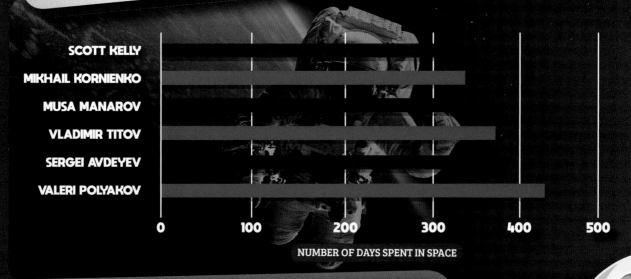

SCOTT KELLY					
MIKHAIL KORNIENKO					
MUSA MANAROV					
VLADIMIR TITOV					
SERGEI AVDEYEV					
VALERI POLYAKOV					

0   100   200   300   400   500

NUMBER OF DAYS SPENT IN SPACE

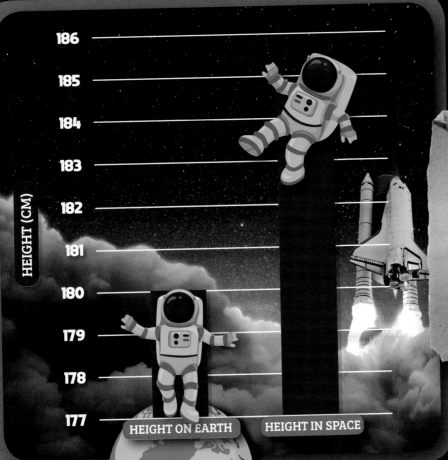

HEIGHT (CM)

186
185
184
183
182
181
180
179
178
177

HEIGHT ON EARTH   HEIGHT IN SPACE

While in space, people grow up to five centimetres (cm) taller than they are on Earth. This is because Earth's gravity is much weaker up in space than it is on Earth's surface.

SHOOTING STARS

METEORS

Have you ever looked up at the sky at night and seen something bright shoot across the sky? Maybe you've even seen lots of these at once. You might know these as shooting stars, but did you know that they're not actually stars at all? Shooting stars are meteors. Meteoroids are pieces of rock and **DEBRIS** in space. Sometimes meteoroids enter Earth's atmosphere, and this is when they become meteors. Meteors travel so quickly that they burn up as they fly through the atmosphere. This creates a long tail of fire that looks like a streak of light across the sky. This is the shooting star! A few times a year, Earth travels past hundreds of meteoroids in one go, which enter our atmosphere and shoot across the sky to produce something called a meteor shower.

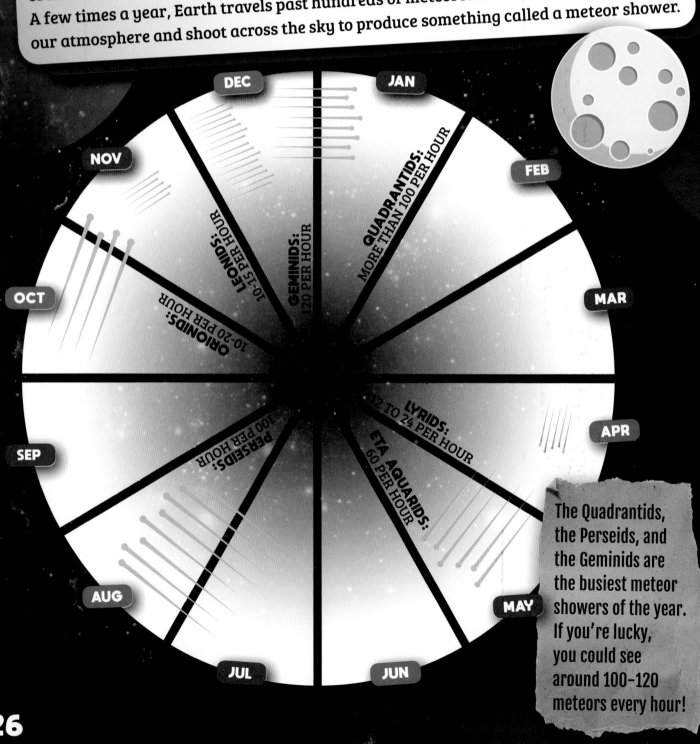

DEC | JAN | FEB | MAR | APR | MAY | JUN | JUL | AUG | SEP | OCT | NOV

QUADRANTIDS: MORE THAN 100 PER HOUR

GEMINIDS: 120 PER HOUR

LEONIDS: 10-15 PER HOUR

ORIONIDS: 10-20 PER HOUR

LYRIDS: 22 TO 24 PER HOUR

ETA AQUARIDS: 60 PER HOUR

PERSEIDS: 100 PER HOUR

The Quadrantids, the Perseids, and the Geminids are the busiest meteor showers of the year. If you're lucky, you could see around 100-120 meteors every hour!

COMETS

Comets are balls of dust, ice, and snow that orbit the Sun. If they get too close to the Sun, they get very hot and the snow and ice begins to melt and boil. The snow and ice quickly turn to gas and create one of the comet's two tails, called a coma. The other tail is made up of the comet's dust.

Comets are usually found very far away from the Sun at the edge of the solar system, so their orbits can be hundreds of years long. Because of this, comets are usually very rare and aren't seen too often.

Halley's Comet is the most famous comet. Because of its orbit around the Sun, it can be seen every 76 years. Halley's Comet was last seen in 1986 but has been recorded by scientists and astronomers since 240 B.C.

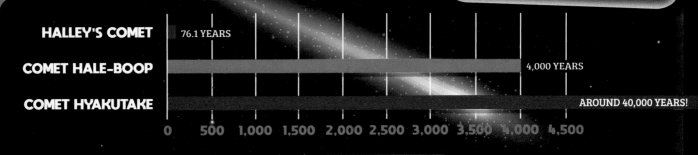

HALLEY'S COMET	76.1 YEARS	
COMET HALE-BOOP		4,000 YEARS
COMET HYAKUTAKE		AROUND 40,000 YEARS!

0   500   1,000   1,500   2,000   2,500   3,000   3,500   4,000   4,500

ORBITAL PERIOD (YEARS)

Just like the planets in our solar system, comets also have different orbital periods around the Sun. Some take a few years to orbit the Sun, but others such as Comet Hyakutake can take around 40,000 years!

DEEP SPACE

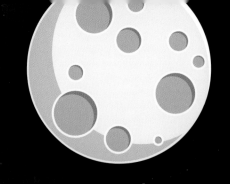

BLACK HOLES

Many things in space, such as dark energy and dark matter, are still a mystery to scientists around the world. Black holes are one of the biggest mysteries of all, and no one is really sure exactly what they are or how they work.

Black holes can be created when galaxies are forming or when a supergiant star explodes and then collapses in on itself. Black holes created from supergiant stars are called stellar black holes. Black holes can usually be found at the centre of nearly all galaxies. In fact, there is a supermassive black hole – the largest type of black hole – at the middle of our galaxy, the Milky Way.

When black holes are formed, all of the matter around it is squeezed into a tiny, very dense point called the singularity. A black hole's gravity is so strong that nothing can escape from it. Even light gets sucked into a black hole and trapped there forever. Because of this, black holes are invisible; it's even impossible to see them through the most powerful telescopes that scientists have.

Anything that gets too close to a black hole is sucked in by its strong gravity. Once something enters a black hole, it can never escape. This pie chart is all one colour — it shows that nothing can escape a black hole.

100%

○ THINGS THAT CAN ESCAPE A BLACK HOLE
● THINGS THAT CAN'T ESCAPE A BLACK HOLE

Because black holes are invisible, it can be very difficult for scientists and astronomers to study them. To learn more about black holes, scientists look at the effect that black holes have on the things around them, such as stars and galaxies.

ACTIVITY: GET SMART!

As the Moon orbits Earth, the amount of it that we can see changes every day. On some days, we might be able to see only a tiny slice of the Moon – this is called a crescent Moon. Other times, the Moon might appear in the sky as a full circle – this is called a full Moon. Try tracking the Moon and drawing pictures of what it looks like for two months. How does it change? Does it ever disappear completely? Use your drawings to create a line graph of the Moon's cycle.

Does your line graph of the Moon's cycle look a bit like this one? Is the shape of the line similar?

THE MOON CYCLE

PERCENTAGE

PERCENT VISIBLE

100
80
60
40
20
0

TIME (DAYS)

GLOSSARY

ASTRONOMERS	people who study the universe and objects in space
ATMOSPHERE	the mixture of gases that make up the air and surround the Earth
ATOM	the smallest part of a chemical element, which is made up of even smaller particles
AXIS	the internal line around which an object spins, such as a planet or moon
B.C.	meaning 'before Christ', it is used to mark dates that occurred before the starting year of most calendars
COSMONAUTS	Russian or Soviet astronauts
CRATERS	large and shallow holes in a planet or moon that are usually caused by a meteorite impact
CYCLE	a series of events that repeat in a circular pattern
DEBRIS	the remains of anything that has been broken down or destroyed
DENSE	tightly packed
DIAMETER	the distance through the centre of an object
DIM	not bright or shiny
DWARF PLANETS	things that orbit a star and are larger than asteroids but smaller than planets
ELLIPTICAL	egg-shaped; like a squashed sphere
FORCE	a push or pull on an object
GAS	an air-like substance that expands freely to fill any space available
GRAVITY	the force that attracts physical bodies together and increases in strength as a body's mass increases
INTERPRET	to understand or work out
LIGHT YEARS	how far light travels in a year. One light year is around 9.5 trillion kilometres
MASS	the amount of matter that a body or object contains
MATTER	substances from which things are made
OBSERVABLE UNIVERSE	the parts of the universe we can see because its light has had time to reach us
ORBITAL PERIOD	the time it takes for something to complete one orbit around another object
PARTICLES	extremely small pieces of a substance
POSITIVE CORRELATION	a relationship between two sets of data where they increase or decrease together
SPACE PROBE	an unmanned spacecraft that can send data back to Earth
WEATHER BALLOON	a balloon that can be sent into the atmosphere to record information about the weather

INDEX